S0-DJM-166

SURVIVING

TEMPTATION Island

DAN & DAVE DAVIDSON
WITH GEORGE VERWER

NEW LEAF PRESS

ISBN: 0-89221-506-2
Library of Congress Number: 2001087476

Unless otherwise noted, Bible Scripture is from the
New International Version® used by permission by Zondervan Publishing House.
All rights reserved © 1973, 1978, 1984 by International Bible Society

Cover Design by: Farewell Communications
Interior Artwork by: Nancy Daniel

Printed in the United States of America.

Please visit our website for other great titles: www.newleafpress.net

For information regarding publicity and author interviews,
please contact Dianna Fletcher at (870) 438-5288.

For complete bibliography, please visit www.SurvivingTemptation.com

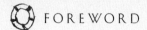 FOREWORD

The Bible has an awful lot to say about temptation, sex, lust, greed, spiritual warfare, and remaining pure. God gives us specific advice on how to avoid temptation and how to escape it when we find ourselves eyeball to eyeball with it.

Dan and Dave Davidson have birthed a lot of books but none more important than *Surviving Temptation Island*. Dave, showing his usual insight and humor asks a hypothetical question: "Who needs to read this book? Anyone with a bellybutton!" I say amen to that.

The reader will be able to measure his or her purity walk with the four Spirit-Flesh zones: Devotion, Destruction, Depletion, and Depravity. Are you sustaining your spirit or feeding your flesh? There is insight for intervention for those entangled in habitual sin and a strong foundation of prevention for everyone's daily walk of purity.

The book is anchored with Scripture in order as it appears in the Bible. You will see how God's Word is the answer to surviving temptation. You will learn from Jesus when He faced temptation. When the Son of God was approached by the tempter in the desert, He did not arm wrestle or debate with the devil. Jesus pulled out the "Sword of the Spirit," which is the Word of God. Jesus said "It is written."

Jesus quoted Scripture and let the power of God's Word hack the tempter's lies to pieces. Victory came by knowing the Word of God and using it. This survival strategy worked for Jesus and works for us today.

This book has taught or re-taught me many things: 1. I need to have a healthy fear (respect, reverence of God.) 2. I have to understand that Satan is directly and creatively waging war against me. 3. God wants to empower me and teach me to walk in holiness and victory.

4. The Holy Spirit helps me in my weakness and provides a way of escape. 5. I must learn God's Word and hide it in my heart "that I might not sin against Him."

Surviving Temptation Island will leave the reader with hope. There is a way to stand. There is a way to avoid temptation. There is a way to survive persistent attacks of the evil one. It is God's way.

Dr. Quigg Lawrence, pastor — Church of the Holy Spirit

AUTHOR INTRODUCTION

Your love life doesn't have to be shipwrecked. You don't have to be a brokenhearted castaway. Purity is not only possible, it is God's plan and provision for you.

No matter what circumstance you're in now — no matter what you've done in the past, God is ready, willing, and able to rescue and restore you. He wants you to experience His forgiveness, hope, and blessing today.

God is the creator of love and sex. He wants us all to understand and take part in His design for purity. We humbly present this book to men and women who want to get right with God. We pray that you will take the biblical truths to heart and honor God with your body and mind. You can reap His rewards rather than sin's consequences.

It's time to meet the challenge to keep pure by living by God's Word. Stand strong amidst temptations that try to pull us down like quicksand.

Take the P.U.R.I.T.Y. pledge and think wow about God's plan of purity in your love life. Take God up on His promises!

Dan & Dave Davidson & George Verwer

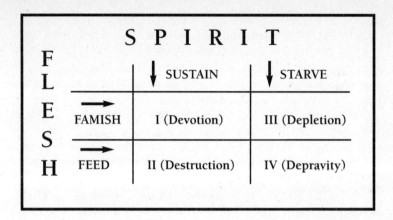

	S P I R I T	
F	↓ SUSTAIN	↓ STARVE
L		
E → FAMISH	I (Devotion)	III (Depletion)
S		
H → FEED	II (Destruction)	IV (Depravity)

The winner in the battle between spirit and flesh is determined by which one gets fed the most. We need to actively sustain our spirit with prayer, study and meditation of God's Word, and fellowship with believers. We also need to do whatever it takes to famish the flesh and its evil desires.

It is a daily challenge of faith. When we do sustain the spirit and famish the flesh, we walk in God's light with wholehearted devotion. We experience a rewarding and fulfilling relationship with Christ and victory over temptation.

I. DEVOTION: Sustaining the Spirit and Famishing the Flesh

Here is where the fruits of the spirit are reflected in your life. The joy of the Lord becomes your strength. It is what Christ had in mind when He said He came to give us abundant life. This is the safe dwelling place of the Lord.

II. DESTRUCTION: Sustaining the Spirit and Feeding the Flesh

This is a battle zone that fans the flames of temptation and spiritual warfare. As long as you try to serve both God and the world there will be internal conflict. Believers often backslide as they continue to feed their flesh.

III. DEPLETION: Starving the Spirit and Famishing the Flesh

Many in this zone try to empty their heart and soul in an attempt to find harmony and inner peace. The result is often a meaningless spiritual void. New age philosophies and eastern religions have their roots here.

IV. DEPRAVITY: Starving the Spirit and Feeding the Flesh

This zone is the home of evil, wickedness, and immorality. Without a godly foundation many give in to the cravings of the sinful nature, following its desires. This condition was reflected in Sodom and Gomorrah.

Sex is the highest physical
act of love between two people to show
their union in spirit, which is a
covenant relationship.

Edwin Louis Cole

For this reason a man will leave his father and
mother and be united to his wife, and they will become
one flesh. The man and his wife were both naked,

and they felt no shame.

Genesis 2:24–25

CHARACTER
IS WHAT YOU ARE
IN THE DARK.

D.L. Moody

Like Eve, we're always looking for something
more, something that will give us more pleasure,

MORE GRATIFICATION.

And like Eve, we're vulnerable to deception.

Bill Perkins

Now the
SERPENT WAS MORE CRAFTY
than any of the wild animals the Lord God had made.
He said to the woman, "Did God really say,
'You must not eat from any tree in the garden'?"
. . . When the woman saw that the fruit of the tree
was good for food and pleasing to the eye,
AND ALSO DESIRABLE
for gaining wisdom,
she took some and ate it.
Genesis 3:1–7

If you do what is right, will you not be accepted?

But if you do not do what is right, sin is crouching at your door;

IT DESIRES TO HAVE YOU,
but you MUST master it.

Genesis 4:7

TEMPTATION suggests the notion of a seduction of sorts,
a drawing of the fly to the spider web . . .
men and women usually do not think seriously
enough about three things:
the strange curiosity within that draws one toward the web,
the entangling potential of the web itself,
and the spider who uses the web
for its own selfish design.

Gordon MacDonald

She caught Joseph by his garment saying,

lie with me;

but he left his garment
in her hand and fled.

Genesis 39:12

MY HERO is Joseph
who RESISTED sin and
maintained sexual purity — He SURVIVED temptation.

George Verwer

YOU SHALL NOT COMMIT ADULTERY.

EXODUS 20:14

Staying faithful doesn't involve just
not sleeping with someone other than your spouse.
It means putting your best effort and energy into
enhancing the romance you have with your mate.
Faithfulness is more than just saying "no"
to others; it's also saying "yes" to your spouse.

Steve & Annie Chapman

It is important for us to exercise
maturity in the choices we make — especially

IN OUR CHOICE OF A MATE.

We cannot afford to be driven by lust or to choose a
companion merely on the basis of some external attribute.

T.D. Jakes

There is no one holy like the Lord;
there is no one besides you;

THERE IS NO ROCK LIKE OUR GOD.

1 Samuel 2:2

REWARD IN THE LORD

**The Lord rewards every man for his
righteousness and faithfulness.**

1 Samuel 26:23

Our bodies are vehicles through which we are to bring honor

and serve God and bring Him glory. What we do with our

bodies impacts our spirits and that impacts eternity.

Tony and Lois Evans

**. . . for the Lord SEARCHES all hearts,
and UNDERSTANDS
           every intent of the THOUGHTS.**

1 Chronicles 28:9

L - LOOK TO GOD. Hebrews 12:2
U - UPROOT SECRET SIN. Jeremiah 16:17
S - SEARCH YOUR HEART. Psalm 139:23
T - TURN AWAY AND REPENT. Ezekiel 14:6
B - BATTLE WITH CHRIST. 2 Corinthians 10:4-5
U - UNITE WITH BELIEVERS. Hebrews 3:1
S - STAND ON GOD'S WORD. 2 Timothy 3:16-17
T - TRIUMPH OVER TEMPTATION. Mark 14:38
E - ESCAPE GOD'S WAY. 1 Corinthians 10:13
R - RENEW YOUR MIND. Romans 12:2
S - STAY THE COURSE. Hebrews 12:1

Dan Davidson

The Lord does not look at the things man looks at.
Man looks at the outward appearance,
but the Lord looks at the heart.

1 Samuel 16:7

IF YOUR CONCEPTION OF LOVE

DOES NOT AGREE WITH JUSTICE AND JUDGMENT

AND PURITY AND HOLINESS,

THEN YOUR IDEA OF LOVE IS WRONG.

Oswald Chambers

Living Below the Balcony

Where do you hang out when it comes to sexual desires? King David spent too much time out on a balcony overlooking Bathsheba's bathing room.

Second Samuel 11:2 describes the situation: *"One evening David got up from his bed and walked around on the roof of the palace. From the roof he saw a woman bathing. The woman was very beautiful."*

The rest of the story . . . David gave in to temptation in a big way. It was the king's actions that put him in a place of temptation to begin with. He *"got up"* and he *"walked around"* and then he *"saw"* a woman bathing. We need to be more like Joseph who chose victory in a tempting situation. Where you decide to hang out greatly affects your daily walk of purity in the eyes of Jesus.

Dan Davidson

> David should have repented upon the roof, not a year later;
> where he had to be called forth and publicly rebuked.
> If we let the sins pile up and our relationship with God grows faint,
> then we shall regret it bitterly.

George Verwer

The rulers of the Philistines went to her and said, "See if
YOU CAN LURE HIM INTO SHOWING YOU
the secret of his great strength and how we can overpower him
so we may tie him up and subdue him.

Judges 16:5

Samson learned what every man must know.

God is the God of the second and third and fourth chance.

He never gives up on us.

Bill Perkins

Naked
I CAME FROM MY MOTHER'S WOMB,
and naked
I WILL DEPART.
The Lord gave and the Lord has taken away;
may the name of the Lord be praised.

Job 1:21

As long as he can CONFUSE YOU and BLIND YOU with his DARK LIES,
you won't be able to see that the chains which once BOUND YOU are broken.
Satan's first and foremost strategy is deception . . . you have to out-truth him.
BELIEVE, DECLARE, and ACT UPON THE TRUTH OF GOD'S WORD,
and you will thwart Satan's strategy.

Neil Anderson

I made a covenant with my eyes
NOT TO LOOK LUSTFULLY AT A GIRL. . . .
Does he not see my ways and count my every step?

Job 31:1–4

There's a dangerous side to the
magnetic appeal of a woman's body,
a side that has the power to enslave a man, the power
to make him do things that violate everything he believes
to be right and good, the power to destroy him and those he loves.

Bill Perkins

PRAY THESE PSALMS TO GOD FOR YOUR SPOUSE

**May he be enthroned in God's presence forever;
appoint your love and faithfulness to protect him.**

Psalm 61:7

**But you, O Lord, are a compassionate and gracious God,
slow to anger, abounding in love and faithfulness.**

Psalm 86:15

**For the Lord is good and his love endures forever;
his faithfulness continues through all generations.**

Psalm 100:5

**Not to us, O Lord, not to us but to your name
be the glory, because of your love and faithfulness.**

Psalm 115:1

WHY HIDE A SECRET SIN?

It only leads to more secrets. You can't
hide from an all-knowing God.

Dave Davidson

You have set our iniquities before you,

our secret sin

in the light of your presence.

Psalm 90:8

*The scriptures urge us to become open. I pray you will be open
about your problems . . . being open, being honest, being in the light.*

George Verwer

What do we think about

when there's nobody around to impress? Where do our fantasies take us? Do we engage in sensual or self-gratifying daydreams? If so, we are programming ourselves for defeat.

Denny Gunderson

Guide me in your truth

and teach me, for you are God my Savior, and my **hope is in you** all day long. . . . **Guard my life and rescue me;** let me not be put to shame, for I take refuge in you.

Psalm 25:5–20

Somebody may come up to you and say,

"Man, are you still single?

You must be REALLY LONELY. Are you ever going to get married?"
You just smile and look at them with great confidence and say,
"Listen, my steps are ordered by the Lord. Psalm 37:4 says,
Because I delight myself in the Lord, He will give me the desires of my heart.

So I don't have anything to worry about."

Joel Osteen

Remember not the sins of my youth and my rebellious ways;
ACCORDING TO YOUR LOVE
remember me, for you are good, O Lord.

Psalm 25:7

DELIGHT YOURSELF IN THE LORD

and he will give you the desires of your heart.

Psalm 37:4

*The best and most beautiful
things in the world cannot be seen
or even touched — they must
be felt with the heart.*

Helen Keller

Create in me a pure heart,

O God, and renew a steadfast spirit within me.
Do not cast me from your presence or take your
Holy Spirit from me. Restore to me the joy of your
salvation and grant me a willing spirit, to sustain me.

Psalm 51:10–12

*King David had an adulterous affair,
got his mistress pregnant
and then arranged to kill her husband.
There were some tough consequences, but David truly repented
and God forgave him. If He forgave David,*

GOD WILL FORGIVE YOU.

Dan Davidson

Satisfied Desires

Praise the Lord who satisfies your desires with good
things so that your youth is renewed like the eagle's.
Psalm 103:5

God created us with emotions and desires. We have a hunger and a thirst for life that seeks to be quenched. While we still live in the world, our daily challenge will remain to satisfy our desires in godly ways.

God's plan is for us to satisfy our desires with good things. Our strength is then renewed like the eagle's. God's Word tells us that *when we hunger and thirst after righteousness, we are blessed.*

On the contrary, when we hunger and thirst after the things of the world — lust, pride, envy, power, etc. — we miss out on God's divine blessings.

How will you quench your thirst for life today?   Dan Davidson

29

How can a young man keep his way pure?

BY LIVING ACCORDING TO YOUR WORD.
I seek you with all my heart; do not let me stray
from your commands. I have hidden your word
in my heart that I might not sin against you.

Psalm 119:9–11

*God's dream for each and every one of you is
that you would come out of the adversity you're in*
**stronger, more mature, with a
greater confidence in God and His Word.**

Joel Osteen

TURN MY EYES AWAY
FROM WORTHLESS THINGS;

PRESERVE MY LIFE ACCORDING TO YOUR WORD.

Psalm 119:37

Don't devote your soul to the remote control.

Dan & Dave Davidson

PURITY,

in its essence, is a reflection of God's character and presence in our lives. To the extent that we live in sexual purity, we reflect for the whole world that God is at work within us, shaping our desires, choices, and actions more than just hormones.

Jerry Kirk

I wait for the Lord,
MY SOUL WAITS,
and in his word I put my hope.
Psalm 130:5

DISCRETION WILL PROTECT YOU,
AND **UNDERSTANDING** WILL GUARD YOU.
Proverbs 2:11

The Lord grants wisdom
and he gives good sense to the godly.
He shows how to distinguish
RIGHT FROM WRONG
and to make the right decision every time.

Proverbs 2:6

Above all else,
GUARD
YOUR
HEART,
for it is the wellspring of life.

Proverbs 4:23

I've learned as a young Christian
not to trust myself. I can't just nibble off the

CHOCOLATE BAR

of pornography and expect to survive the battle.
Some of us are pornaholics. I don't say this lightly.
We need to stay away from this stuff!

George Verwer

*It is time to realize that there is no such thing as a completely
satisfied person. Otherwise, there would be no need for heaven.
We only get a piece of the pie. There is always something
more that we want out of life that we cannot have.*

Tony Campolo

Spiritual Blinders

Horse trainers have learned over the years the importance of using blinders on a horse during a race. The primary focus is the path of the track ahead. Victory would be impossible without the use of blinders because horses are so easily distracted.

The race of life is not much different for us. If our eyes are not fixed on Jesus, evil things of the world can easily distract us. Because of our old sinful nature, we need God's spiritual blinders to prevent us from swerving into sin.

The decisions we make in our race of life determine our eternal address. The prize is fellowship with Jesus and an eternity of heavenly rewards. *Dan Davidson*

Let your eyes look straight ahead,

fix your gaze directly before you. Make level paths for your feet
and take only ways that are firm. Do not swerve to the right or the left;

keep your foot from evil.

Proverbs 4:25–27

THINK ABOUT
what you're
THINKING ABOUT.
Examine your THOUGHT life regularly.

Joel Osteen

Like a gold ring in a pig's snout is a
beautiful woman who shows no discretion.

Proverbs 11:22

He who works his land will have abundant food,
but he who chases fantasies lacks judgment.

Proverbs 12:11

Sinning
while thinking there will be no
eventual consequence
is like sky diving without a parachute
and assuming you will
simply
drift
down
safely.   Dave Davidson

DO NOT lust in your heart after her beauty or let her captivate you with her eyes. . . . Can a man scoop fire into his lap without his clothes being burned? Can a man walk on hot coals without his feet being scorched? . . . DO NOT LET YOUR HEART TURN TO HER WAYS OR STRAY INTO HER PATHS.

Proverbs 6:25–7:25

I have NEVER met a man who

waited until marriage

for sexual intimacy and then REGRETTED the choice.
But I've met hundreds who regretted
their premarital sexual encounters.

Jerry Kirk

Jesus challenged us not to add onto the God-given
sexual drive by polluting our minds with lustful thoughts.

The only way to control your sexual life is to control

YOUR THOUGHT LIFE.

Neil Anderson

The deepest pleasures in life

don't satisfy — they point us forward.
Until we attain unity with Christ in heaven,
an inconsolable longing for more
will remain in every human heart.

Larry Crabb

A longing fulfilled is a tree of life.
Hope deferred makes the heart sick.

Proverbs 13:12

Patience and restraint may be the highest expression of love.

Tony Campolo

YOUR CONSCIENCE
is like a built-in
LIE DETECTOR.

We must always pray for discernment.
Through it God gives us the
confidence of His hope.

Dave Davidson

There is a way that seems right to a
man, but in the end it leads to death.

Proverbs 14:12 & 16:25

He who finds

A WIFE

FINDS WHAT IS GOOD
and receives favor from the Lord.

Proverbs 18:22

Curiosity has killed more marriages than cats.

Dave Davidson

Many a man claims to have unfailing love,
but a faithful man who can find?

Proverbs 20:6

IS IT FITTING?

Is it in accord with the pattern I'd like my life to follow?
Does it harmonize with my best understanding of God's plan?
What is it that brings God's man and God's woman
near to each other with delicacy and grace?
Do I want to walk, here as in all areas of my life,
by faith, or will I take things into my own hands?

Elizabeth Elliot

42

I'VE THOUGHT ABOUT MANY THINGS,

but the most awesome, the most terrifying,
the most shattering thought I've ever had,
is my personal accountability to God one day.

Daniel Webster

GOD'S CHATROOM

......memo from the creator of love & sex......

*I can restore you and make you whole. Do you believe that? Take heart, I am
with you always. You can always trust in Me. If there is anyone you can trust it is Me.
I created you and I created sex to be a dynamic blessing for you in marriage.
No matter where you are today in your relationships, I can bless you and
give you the grace and peace and love for which you have been searching.
Depend and trust in My power and guidance.*

Your Loving and Creative Father, God in Heaven

TALKING WITH JESUS

Dear Jesus,
Thanks for not only loving me enough to restore me,
but also giving the gift of love and sex.
I want to see these gifts appropriately
through Your eyes and not the world's.
Remind me again and again
of the importance of following You,
clinging to You in trust
and putting my hope
in You.

44

Whether it be soap operas,

ROMANCE NOVELS,

or supermodel dreams, as long as we're
focused on a distraction contrary to God's
will, we become vulnerable to subtle slips of
sin. The sin of lasciviousness deals with being
willing to sin, with or without the opportunity.
God is concerned about motives of the heart
while the devil wants you sidelined at any cost.

Dave Davidson

Who can say, "I have kept my heart pure;
I am clean and without sin"?

Proverbs 20:9

Farmer in a Rut

Do not eat the bread of a selfish man, or desire his
delicacies; for as he thinks within himself, so he is.
Proverbs 23:6–7

You are what you eat, right? What about in the attitudes of the heart?
Since our secret thought life is the basis for our actions, it is here where
entertaining thoughts can become seeds for the future. The wrong habits can
create a groove much like falling into a rut. Denny Gunderson tells this story:
Picture a farmer driving his tractor down a dirt road. When the road is new, the
smooth grade allows the farmer to easily drive from side to side. But if the farmer
constantly drives in the same place, ruts or grooves begin to form in the road and
it becomes increasingly difficult to steer his tractor. Eventually, if the road isn't
smoothed over, the ruts become so deep that the tractor tires just naturally
follow them.

Where is the groove that your thought life resembles? Is it hard to
escape the ditch of fleshly habits? Is it time to clear the ruts in your life?
Pray that God will rain down His restoration to smooth over the dirt road and
make new trails of freedom in Christ for you.

Dave Davidson

PRACTICING SEXUAL PURITY,

even though it's hard, is also one of the most accurate reflections of the depth of our relationship with Christ.

Jerry Kirk

WE DON'T
"FALL" INTO SIN,
WE *SLIDE* INTO IT.

Ken Williams

Our eyes don't have to be wandering to fall into traps of lust. We must remember the enemy is always trying to steal, kill, and destroy every

good relationship

in our life. Only God's truth revealed in His Word can protect us from the devil's steady onslaught of temptation. That is why we must ask for God's strength to guard our hearts day and night.

Dan Davidson

As water reflects a face,
so a man's heart reflects the man.

Proverbs 27:19

48

A wife of noble character

who can find? She is worth far more than
rubies. Her husband has full confidence
in her and lacks nothing of value.

Proverbs 31:10–11

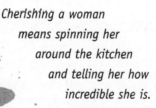

*Cherishing a woman
means spinning her
around the kitchen
and telling her how
incredible she is.*

Becca Lynn

GOD INTENDS . . . that the "one flesh" experience
should be an expression and a heightening of
the partner's sense that, being given to each other,
they now belong together, each needing the
other for COMPLETION AND WHOLENESS.

J. I. Packer

Charm is deceptive, and beauty is fleeting;
but a woman who fears the Lord is to be praised.

Proverbs 31:30

CHARM CAN BE AN ALARM,
which sounds when love begins lying and lust starts trying to barge in.

Dave Davidson

 **MARRIAGE**
IS LIKE A LONG TRIP
IN A TINY ROWBOAT.
If one passenger starts to rock the boat, the
other passenger has to steady it — otherwise,
they'll go to the bottom together.

Dr. David Reuban

Two are better than one, because they
have a good return for their work: If one falls down,
his friend can help him up. But pity the man who
falls and has no one to help him up!

Ecclesiastes 4:9–10

Enjoy life with your wife,

whom you love, all the days.

Ecclesiastes 9:9

Unless you lovingly and energetically
NURTURE YOUR MARRIAGE,
you will begin to drift away from your mate.

Dennis Rainey

*The old Christian rule is either marriage, with complete faithfulness
to your partner, or else total abstinence.*

C.S. Lewis

Remember your Creator in the
days of your youth,
before the days of trouble come and the years approach
when you will say, "I find no pleasure in them." . . . Now
all has been heard; here is the conclusion of the matter:
Fear God and keep his commandments,
for this is the whole duty of man. For God will bring
every deed into judgment,
including every hidden thing, whether it is good or evil.

Ecclesiastes 12:1–14

Even the young and the brave can be fooled
by the shenanigans of runaway emotions.

James Dobson

My lover spoke and said to me,
"Arise, my darling, my beautiful one,
and come with me. See! The winter is past;
the rains are over and gone. Flowers appear
on the earth; the season of singing has come. . . .
Arise, come, my darling;
my beautiful one, come with me."

Song of Songs 2:10–13

FOR WOMEN, FOR SOME MEN,
tenderness, touching, talking, and sex go together.
sex is sufficient, especially if they do not know how to relate in other forms of intimacy.

H. Norman Wright

If virginity

is to be preserved, lines must be drawn.
Why put yourself in any situation where the lines become
smudged and obscure? Why take risks? Why accept the
pressure of tremendous temptation when you can easily avoid
it by refusing to be anywhere where compromise is possible?

Elizabeth Elliot

*Are you no longer a virgin
and have just realized what you have lost and would
desire to have it back? You may not get it back physically,
but you can mentally, emotionally, and spiritually.*
God will restore the spirit and glory
of it to your life if you ask Him.

Edwin Louis Cole

Catch for us the foxes, the little foxes that ruin the vineyards,
our vineyards that are in bloom. . . .

Daughters of Jerusalem,

I charge you by the gazelles and by the does of the field:
Do not arouse or awaken love until it so desires.

Song of Songs 2:15–3:5

Intimacy
IS ABOUT OPENING UP

and revealing ourselves to another.
It's not about manipulating another to fulfill our fantasies.
Intimacy is about caring for another's pleasure as much or more
than we care about our own. It's not about seeing another as just a tool
to bring us pleasure. . . . Intimacy is about cherishing another in ways
that go far beyond sex. It's not about seeing that person as disposable
when the demands of everyday life put a crimp on sexual escapades.

Laurie Hall

HOW DO I LOVE THEE?
LET ME BE ACCOUNTABLE TO THY WAYS.
Dave Davidson

BEING ACCOUNTABLE

Many godly people have become entangled in sexual sin because they had no one holding them accountable for their physical relationship. . . . If we need help maintaining some of the basic disciplines of the Christian life, how much more will we need the help of our brothers and sisters as we seek to channel the tumultuous currents of our sexual appetites? Admitting our need for help in this area is definitely humbling and sometimes embarrassing. But it is also essential as we seek to honor God in our relationships.

Valerie Gladu

LOVE can wait
and worship endlessly;
lust says, "I must have it at once."

Oswald Chambers

Kissing, like salt water, seems quenching
yet leaves those exposed with a deeper thirst.

Dave Davidson

Your lips are like a scarlet ribbon; your mouth is lovely.
Until the day breaks and the shadows flee. . . . All beautiful
you are, my darling; there is no flaw in you.

Song of Songs 4:3–6

Sensual pleasure
passes and vanishes in the twinkling of an eye,
but the friendship between us, the mutual confidence,

the delights of the heart,

the enchantment of the soul,
these things do not perish
and can never be destroyed.
I shall love you until I die.

Voltaire

You have stolen my heart, my sister, my bride;
you have stolen my heart with one glance of
your eyes. . . . How delightful is your love.

Song of Songs 4:9–10

The best part about

beauty

is that which no picture can express.

Francis Bacon

*Thank God we have a creator who gives us the powerful ability
to have and to fulfill sexual desire!*

Dave Davidson

**I am my lover's and my lover is mine;
he browses among the lilies.**

Song of Songs 6:3

INFATUATION

is when you think that he's as sexy as
Robert Redford, as smart as Henry Kissinger,
as noble as Ralph Nader, as funny as Woody Allen,
and as athletic as Jimmy Connors. Love is when you
realize that he's as sexy as Woody Allen, as smart as
Jimmy Connors, as funny as Ralph Nader, as athletic
as Henry Kissinger, and nothing like Robert
Redford — but you'll take him anyway.

Judith Viorst

**How beautiful you are and how pleasing,
O love, with your delights!**

Song of Songs 7:6

Genuine love

*motivates us to build a relationship primarily
for the other person's sake, and when we do that,
we gain because we have a better relationship to enjoy.*

Gary Smalley

THE TYPE OF HUMAN BEING WE PREFER
REVEALS THE CONTOURS OF OUR HEART.

Ortega Y. Gasset

The mandrakes send out their fragrance,
and at our door is every delicacy, both new and old,
that I have stored up for you, my lover.

Song of Songs 7:13

Place me like a seal over your heart,
like a seal on your arm; for love is as strong
as death, its jealousy unyielding as the grave.

It burns like blazing fire,

like a mighty flame. Many waters cannot
quench love; rivers cannot wash it away.

Songs of Songs 8:6–7

WE ARE SHAPED AND FASHIONED
BY WHAT WE LOVE.

Goethe

63

Voices are saying, "Let it all hang out," and "Tell it like it is," and "Hold nothing back," and "Be open . . . express your feeling without restraint!" It's easy to buy that kind of advice. But when I go to my Bible, I find contrary counsel being marketed.

Charles Swindoll

Don't let some cheap, tawdry relationship

in the back of a van,

or at a cheap motel, or on a sandy beach blanket,
or in hushed whispers in the living room,
rob you of the greatest moment of your life!

Edwin Louis Cole

"Come now, let us reason together," says the Lord.
"Though your sins are like scarlet, they shall be as

WHITE AS SNOW;

though they are red as crimson, they shall be like wool."

Isaiah 1:18

TEMPTATION is the **TEMPTER**
looking through the keyhole into the room
where **YOU** are living;
SIN is your drawing back the bolt
and making it possible for him to **ENTER.**

J. Wilbur Chapman

I know some of you right now are FACING TREMENDOUS DIFFICULTIES
and you're struggling. And maybe it feels like the whole world has
come AGAINST YOU. Well, friends, you've got to start to
DWELL ON ISAIAH 54:17 all week long. It says,
"NO WEAPON THAT IS FORMED AGAINST YOU IS GOING TO PROSPER."
When those negative thoughts come your way, you just REJECT THEM
and you say, "No, devil, you may have formed this weapon against me,
but in the NAME OF JESUS, God promises me — He guarantees it
is not going to prosper and in the end, I will OVERCOME."
See, the Bible says, "When you've done everything
you know to do to just STAND ON THE PROMISES OF GOD."
Just dwell on the fact that you are

MORE THAN A CONQUEROR.

Joel Osteen

Drawing the Line

I will make justice the measuring line
and righteousness the plumb line.
Isaiah 28:17

A young toddler had repeatedly run out into the street to chase a ball. His mom decided to use some sidewalk chalk to draw a line near the end of the driveway to show her son how far he could run after his ball without risking the danger of oncoming traffic.

In the same way God has drawn divine lines in His Word that reflect boundaries of holiness and righteousness. A good place to start is the Ten Commandments. These are clear-cut measuring lines from God that protect us and keep us in the safe dwelling place of the Lord.

As you come to know Christ more intimately, pray that God's plumb lines would be revealed to you. Determine the divine, then draw the line.

Once you know what God's standards are, you need to draw lines for your life that match God's holy plumb lines. How do you measure up?

Dan Davidson

67

WHEN WE CROSS THE BOUNDARIES

set by God for our well-being, we choose a path that,
while sometimes pleasurable in the short run,
undermines our confidence in God and says to Him
that we don't really believe He knows what's best for us.

Jerry Kirk

Going beyond the fences

has to do with outright disobeying the will of Christ
and neglecting the spiritual disciplines given to us for our
maximum protection. When we cross the fence line,
we open the gate to increasing possibilities for broken-world choices.

Gordon MacDonald

There will be a time for these tears
to cease their flow,
for these fears to flow into joy.
We shall be released
from our isolated island states,
from these stone weights
on our wings.

Matt Malyon

. . . but those who hope in the Lord will renew their strength.
They will soar on wings like eagles;
they will run and not grow weary, they will walk and not be faint.

Isaiah 40:31

EROTIC PLEASURE
is the most superficial benefit of sex.
It is a delight, but only the delight of a moment.

John White

"For I know the plans I have for you,"
declares the LORD, "plans to prosper and not
harm you, plans to give you hope and a future."

Jeremiah 29:11

MY TEMPTATIONS
HAVE BEEN MY MASTERS IN DIVINITY.

Martin Luther

What will
it take for you to

WAKE UP

and feel as forgiven as you are?
"Good morning Lord, remind me of
what You've done for me on the cross."

Dave Davidson

Yet this I call to mind and therefore I have hope:
Because of the Lord's great love we are not consumed,
for his compassions never fail. They are new every
morning; great is your faithfulness.

Lamentations 3:21–23

UNCHECKED SIN LEADS TO MORE SIN.

The destructive cycle expands. You can't shut down the longing of a soul.
If that longing is not met in God, it will resurrect itself in any number
of ways: shame, guilt, anger, depression, and of course, more sin:
trying to order the world through selfishness.

Bill Hybels

*Maybe this is stupid, maybe this is wise,
maybe this is cupid, where his arrow lies.*

Dave Davidson

Is no secret hidden from you?

Ezekiel 28:3

72

He reveals deep and hidden things; he knows
what lies in darkness, and light dwells with him.

Daniel 2:22

A boy had his hand stuck in an expensive vase. His father
had to break the vase around the boy's hand only to find
his son holding onto a worthless coin. In the same way we
forfeit God's grace when we hold onto what Bill Perkins calls
"OUR OBJECT OF LUST."

Dave Davidson

Those who cling to worthless idols sacrifice the grace
that could be theirs. But I with a song of thanksgiving will
sacrifice to you. What I have vowed I will make good.

Jonah 2:8–9

If I take care of my character,
my reputation will take care of itself.

D. L. Moody

So guard yourself in your spirit, and do not break faith
with the wife of your youth.

Malachi 2:15

BLESSED ARE THE
PURE IN HEART,
FOR THEY WILL SEE GOD.

Matthew 5:8

But I tell you that anyone who looks at a woman
lustfully has already committed adultery with her in his heart.

Matthew 5:28

Remember that these women
are created in the image of God.
THEY ARE SOMEONE'S DAUGHTERS.
Imagine how you would feel if it was *your* daughter.
Our lust for them keeps them in bondage
and grieves the heart of God, because
THEY ARE HIS DAUGHTERS.

Henry Rogers

And lead us not into TEMPTATION,
but DELIVER US from the evil one.

Matthew 6:13

Lay up treasure in heavenly measure.

Dan & Dave Davidson

For where your treasure is,
there your heart will be also.

Matthew 6:21

God intended our Pleasure Island to be

His Treasure Island.

It depends on our obedience and faithfulness

to His commands and promises. Don't be fooled by

the devil's version of Temptation Island.

Dan Davidson

God's Word is like a
life preserver.
When waves of the world and
the enemy crash against us,
cling to the Word so you
won't be shipwrecked on
Temptation Island.

Dan Davidson

Watch and pray so that you
WILL NOT FALL INTO TEMPTATION.
The spirit is willing, but the body is weak.

Mark 14:38 & Matthew 26:41

Don't be like Gilligan who always missed his chance
to escape the island he was trapped on.

Dave Davidson

More marriages might
SURVIVE
if the partners realized
that sometimes the better
comes after the worse.

Doug Larsen

With unrealistic expectations
your "Love Boat" dream may end up
SINKING LIKE THE TITANIC.

Dave Davidson

**For this reason a man will leave his father and mother
and be united to his wife, and the two will become one flesh.
SO THEY ARE NO LONGER TWO, BUT ONE.
Therefore what God has joined together, let man not separate.**

Mark 10:7–9

FORGIVE US OUR SINS,
for we also forgive everyone who sins against us.
And lead us not into temptation.

Luke 11:4

*TEMPTATION IS SATAN'S TOOL
for getting you to do things that you really don't want to do.
Deep inside your spirit, you know that what he is
TEMPTING YOU TO DO IS WRONG.*

T.D. Jakes

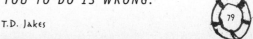

79

Your eye is the lamp of your body.
WHEN YOUR EYES ARE GOOD,
your whole body also is full of light.

Luke 11:34

The thief comes only to steal and kill and destroy;
I have come that they may have life, and have it to the full.

John 10:10

The DEVIL either POUNCES on us like a roaring lion or
he tries prowling like a wolf in sheep's clothing.
Whatever the method, his strategy is always to STEAL,
KILL, and DESTROY the aspect of PURITY in our relationships.

Dan Davidson

Overcoming Power

In the world ye shall have tribulation: but
be of good cheer; I have overcome the world.
John 16:33;KJV

Jesus tells us directly that we will have trials in life. He also encourages us with the eternal reality that He has overcome the world by virtue of His victory on the cross.

The manifestation of this "overcoming" in our lives is similar to the manna from heaven that gave daily sustenance to the Israelites.

Oswald Chambers in his book *My Utmost For His Highest* helps put this divine power in perspective, "God does not give us overcoming life: He gives us life as we overcome. The strain is the strength. If there is no strain, there is no strength.

If you spend yourself out physically, you become exhausted; but spend yourself spiritually, and you get more strength. God never gives strength for tomorrow, or for the next hour, but only for the strain of the minute."

Look to Jesus and he will grant you His overcoming power and grace for whatever trial you are faced with today.   Dan Davidson

We've had the joy of seeing people
SET FREE FROM PORNOGRAPHY AND HOMOSEXUALITY.
Be set free and experience forgiveness and the grace
to run the race even right on out to the mission field.

George Verwer

The time to stop temptation is the moment it
rears its ugly head.

Thomas a. Kempis

God gave them over in the
SINFUL DESIRES OF THEIR HEARTS
to sexual impurity for the degrading of their bodies with one another.

Romans 1:24

Understand and see yourself
AS GOD SEES YOU.
He longs to be in deep relationship
with you and meet your every need.
HE TREASURES YOU
like no one else. He is incapable of damaging
those He loves. All His actions
and thoughts toward you are
designed to make you all
He created you to be.

Bill Hybels

You see, at just the right time, when we were
still powerless, Christ died for the ungodly.
But God demonstrates His own love for us in this:
While we were still sinners, Christ died for us.

Romans 5:6–8

Hope or Hype

And hope does not disappoint us, because God has poured out
his love into our hearts by the Holy Spirit, whom he has given us.
Romans 5:5

There's a big difference between the hope of heaven and the hype of hell. The enemy tempts us with what he portrays as the pleasures of sin. But sin always disappoints. It never lives up to its promise. When we're tempted by sin, it's nothing more than the devil pitching us a package of lies filled with hype.

Christ offers us the true hope of heaven. We are saved by His grace and have become heirs in the kingdom of God. We have been adopted by the Creator of the universe. Titus 3:7 tells us, "Having been justified by his grace, we become heirs having the hope of eternal life."

This promise is not hype at all — it is the truth. It is eternal. A personal relationship with Jesus offers us a daily hope — a hope that the Bible tells us does not disappoint. Don't be fooled by the hype of hell. Put your hope in heaven.

Dan Davidson

Therefore do not let sin reign in your
mortal body so that you obey its evil desires.

Romans 6:12

The mind of sinful man is death, but the
MIND CONTROLLED BY THE SPIRIT IS LIFE AND PEACE;
the sinful mind is hostile to God. It does not submit to God's law,
nor can it do so. Those controlled by the sinful nature cannot please God.

Romans 8:6–8

*To pray against temptation, and yet to rush
into occasion, is to thrust your fingers into the
fire, and then pray they might not be burnt.*

Thomas Secker

PASSION
never naturally leads to purity.
Purity must be priority over passion.

Dave Davidson

If PASSION drives, let reason hold the reins.

Benjamin Franklin

A man in PASSION rides a horse
that runs away with him.

C.H. Spurgeon

Therefore,
I urge you, brothers,
in view of God's mercy, to offer
YOUR BODIES

as living sacrifices, holy and pleasing to
God — this is your spiritual act of worship.

Romans 12:1

Develop the discipline
of not giving up or giving in.

Dan & Dave Davidson

Renew Your Mind

Do not conform any longer to the pattern of this world,
but be transformed by the renewing of your mind.
Romans 12:2

Whether you realize it or not, you are in the midst of a battle. The world is waging war on your mind.

The Bible tells us "we are in the world, but not of the world." While on earth we must be on guard and resist conforming to worldly standards.

What do you do on a regular basis to "renew" your mind? The definition of renew is "to make new again; to restore to freshness, perfection, or vigor; to give new life to; to rejuvenate; to reestablish; to recreate; to rebuild."

We need to retreat, reflect and renew. Take some time away from the hustle and bustle of life to rest. Cancel a meeting; eliminate a responsibility; set aside some quality time with your family.

Spend time in prayer and meditate on God's Word. God is ready to make your mind new again in the image of His Son.

Dan Davidson

Opportunities for temptation come and go,
but by the grace of God, I will hold myself

sexually abstinent

until I marry. For me, my abstinence is more
than a statement. It's a personal conviction.

A. C. Green

LOVE MUST BE SINCERE. . . .

Honor one another above yourselves. . . .
Be joyful in hope, patient in affliction, faithful in prayer.

Romans 12:9–12

LOVE

**is of all the passions the strongest,
for it attacks simultaneously the head, the heart, and the senses.**

Voltaire

Let us behave decently, as in the daytime, not in orgies and
drunkenness, not in sexual immorality and debauchery, not
in dissension and jealousy. Rather, clothe yourselves with
the Lord Jesus Christ, and do not think about how
to gratify the desires of the sinful nature.

Romans 13:13–14

When a man sits with a pretty girl for an hour,
it seems like a minute. But let him sit on a hot stove
for a minute and it's longer than any hour.

That's relativity.

Albert Einstein

Our sexuality is our creative force.

Billy Graham

A WOMAN is sort of like an IRON
and a MAN is like a LIGHT BULB.
She warms up to the sexual expression,
while he turns on immediately.

Gary Smalley

I DO not understand what I DO.
For what I want to do I DO not do, but what I hate I DO. . . .
For what I DO is not the good I want to do;
no, the evil I DO not want to do — this I keep on doing.
Now if I DO what I DO not want to do, it is no longer
I who do it, but it is sin living in me that does it. . . .
Who will rescue me from this body of death?
Thanks be to God — through Jesus Christ our Lord!

Romans 7:15–25

TEMPTATION PROVOKES ME
TO LOOK UPWARD TO GOD.

John Bunyan

If what he has built

SURVIVES

he will receive his reward.

1 Corinthians 3:14

Don't you know that you yourselves are
God's temple and that God's Spirit lives in you?

1 Corinthians 3:16

I am not writing this to shame you,
but to warn you, as my dear children.

1 Corinthians 4:14

Because sex was created by God
TO BE POWERFUL,
the consequences of abusing God's design
ARE NO LESS POWERFUL.

Bill Hybels

When you need to run from evil,
it's always better to turn around,
repent, and start running away,
rather than backing up. If you back-peddle
you may just end up back-sliding.

Dave Davidson

94

Moments of pleasure are the remnants that
WASH ASHORE FROM A SHIPWRECK,
bits of Paradise extended through time.
We must hold gifts lightly, with gratitude,
never seize them as our right and entitlement.

Phillip Yancey

THE BODY

is not meant for immorality, but for the Lord.

1 Corinthians 6:13

Fornication is wrong because it defeats God's purpose for your sexuality.
It replaces the freedom with bondage and closes the door to the
deepest intimacies of all. Your body does not belong to you
but to God whether you call yourself a Christian or not.
Your sexuality is likewise not yours but His. . . . You have
only two options: to be free within God's purposes for you or to
be a slave to sex, to yourself and to the others outside of his purposes.

John White

Tarnished, varnished

my eyes are in an airbrushed harness.
It affects how we see each other . . .
False seed, imagery, corrupting my philosophy,
creates a ladder no one can climb . . .
I fight the battle for my mind.

Matt Malyon

Flee from sexual immorality. All other sins a man commits are outside his body, but he who sins sexually sins against his own body. Do you not know that your body is a temple of the Holy Spirit, who is in you, whom you have received from God? You are not your own; you were bought at a price. Therefore honor God with your body.

1 Corinthians 6:18–20

You are not to blame for the birds that fly over your head,
but if you allow them to come down and make a nest in your hair,
then you are to blame. And so with these evil thoughts
that come flashing into our minds;
we have to fight them.

D. L. Moody

WHEN GOD SAYS "NO,"

it means He wants to protect, preserve, and prepare us
for something better. It means a more fulfilling
"Yes," is waiting right around the corner.
Can you trust God in patience?

Dave Davidson

I am saying this for your own good,
NOT TO RESTRICT YOU,
but that you may live in a right way
in undivided devotion to the Lord.

1 Corinthians 7:35

98

No temptation has seized you except what is common to man.
And God is faithful; he will not let you be tempted beyond what
you can bear. But when you are tempted, he will also provide
a way out so that you can stand up under it.

1 Corinthians 10:13

LOVE is patient, LOVE is kind. It does not envy, it does not boast,
it is not proud. It is not rude, it is not self-seeking, it is not easily angered,
it keeps no record of wrongs. LOVE does not delight in evil but rejoices
with the truth. It always protects, always trusts, always hopes,
always perseveres. LOVE never fails. But where there are prophecies,
they will cease; where there are tongues, they will be stilled; where
there is knowledge, it will pass away. . . . And now these three remain:
faith, hope and LOVE. But the greatest of these is LOVE.

1 Corinthians 13:4–13

Whenever you're tempted,
prayer can be an emergency rescue — a direct flare gun to God.

Dave Davidson

Therefore, my dear brothers, stand firm.
Let NOTHING move you.

1 Corinthians 15:58

Be on your guard;
STAND FIRM
IN THE FAITH;
be men of courage; be strong.
Do everything in love.

1 Corinthians 16:13–14

WE LIVE BY FAITH, NOT BY SIGHT.

2 Corinthians 5:7

Failures for the believer are always temporary.
God loves you and me so much that He will
allow almost any failure if the end result
is that we become more like Jesus.

George Verwer

Nothing liberates a man
from the grip of sin as the intoxicating
discovery that he is freely accepted and forgiven.

John White

GOD IS PROMISING

right now that your fetishes,
your fixations and your fears
will and can be reconciled by Him.
Are you willing to bank on His promises?

Dave Davidson

Since we have these promises, dear friends,
let us purify ourselves from everything that
contaminates body and spirit, perfecting
holiness out of reverence for God.

2 Corinthians 7:1

Captive Thoughts

. . . bringing every thought into captivity to the obedience of Christ,
2 Corinthians 10:5

A man ran past the security checkpoint at Chicago's O'Hare airport in the United Airlines terminal. Instead of passing it off as just a prank, several serious measures were taken to maintain the highest level of security.

Every passenger in the entire United Airlines terminal area was evacuated and then asked to be re-checked through the x-ray security station. There were long delays and many flights ended up being canceled.

To some it may have seemed that these extreme measures were an unnecessary hassle. However, the airline was willing to sacrifice comfort and convenience of passengers to search for the one person who may have posed a threat to everyone's safety.

When we have the mind of Christ, the Holy Spirit acts like an x-ray check point for every thought that attempts to enter our mind. God's Word tells us to "bring every thought into captivity to the obedience of Christ."

Impure thoughts may require extreme measures in order to protect and preserve your heart, soul, and mind. Be ready to stand guard and take captive any thought that does not measure up to the mind of Christ.   Dan Davidson

Moral failure is rarely the result of a
blowout;
Almost always, it's the result of a slow leak.

Gary J. Oliver

But I am afraid that just as Eve was deceived
by the serpent's cunning, your minds may somehow be
led astray from your sincere and pure devotion to Christ.

2 Corinthians 11:3

THE POWER OF IMMORAL SEX CAN DESTROY
US IF WE DON'T TREAT IT LIKE A MORTAL ENEMY.

Steve Farrar

UNDERSTAND
GOD'S GRACE TO FAILURES.

George Verwer

Develop a thirst for faith things first.

Dan & Dave Davidson

But he said to me, "My grace is sufficient for you,
for my power is made perfect in weakness."
Therefore I will boast all the more gladly about

MY WEAKNESSES,
so that Christ's power may rest on me.

2 Corinthians 12:9

Lust, through its filter of selfishness, warps natural, God-given desires. Admiring the grace and beauty of a woman as a unique and wonderful creation of God, when filtered through lust, reduces the woman to an object.

Bill Hybels

EVERY MOMENT OF RESISTANCE TO TEMPTATION IS A VICTORY.

Fredrick William Faber

I have been crucified with Christ and I no longer live, but Christ lives in me. The life I live in the body, **I LIVE BY FAITH IN THE SON OF GOD,** who loved me and gave himself for me.

Galatians 2:20

IT IS FOR **FREEDOM**
THAT CHRIST HAS SET US FREE.

Stand firm, then, and do not let yourselves
be burdened again by a yoke of

SLAVERY. . . .

You were running a good race. Who cut in on you and kept you
from obeying the truth? . . . You, my brothers, were called to be free.
But do not use your freedom to indulge the sinful
nature; rather, serve one another in love.

Galatians 5:1–13

So I say, live by the Spirit, and you will not gratify the desires of the sinful
nature. For the sinful nature desires what is contrary to the Spirit,
and the Spirit what is contrary to the sinful nature.
They are in conflict with each other,
so that you do not do what you want.

Galatians 5:16–17

The acts of the sinful nature are obvious: sexual immorality,
impurity and debauchery. . . . But the fruit of the Spirit is
**LOVE, JOY, PEACE, PATIENCE, KINDNESS, GOODNESS,
FAITHFULNESS, GENTLENESS AND SELF-CONTROL.**
Against such things there is no law.

Galatians 5:19–23

Each temptation requires
YOUR RESPONSIBILITY
and God's ability. God will not do for you what He has
already equipped you to do yourself. And no matter how
hard you try, you cannot do what only He can do.

J. Allan Petersen

SATAN SETS US UP IN ADVANCE.

That's one of his schemes. In many small ways, he tills the ground of our heart so that when he finally sends the big temptation, it takes root in our heart and we fall. That is why being faithful in small things is so important. We must commit to holiness across the board.

David Kyle Foster

**Brothers, if someone is caught in a sin,
you who are spiritual should restore him gently.
But watch yourself, or you also may be tempted.**

Galatians 6:1

Do not be deceived: God cannot be mocked,
A MAN REAPS WHAT HE SOWS.

Galatians 6:7

Let us not become weary in doing good, for at the proper time
we reap a harvest if we do not give up.

Galatians 6:9

I pray that in a deeper way you will
no longer trust yourself,
but what Christ has done for you on the cross.

George Verwer

If we don't immediately identify tempting thoughts and take them captive to what we know to be true — if we don't immediately replace the wrong thinking with the right thinking — we'll become so weak that we won't care what we do until after we've sinned and begun to taste the bitter consequences.

Gary J. Oliver

SIN HAS FOUR CHARACTERISTICS:

Self-sufficiency instead of faith,

Self-will instead of submission,

Self-seeking instead of benevolence;

Self-righteousness instead of humility.

E. Paul Hovey

Having lost all sensitivity, they have given themselves
over to sensuality so as to indulge in every kind of
impurity, with a continual lust for more.

Ephesians 4:19

You were taught, with regard to your former way of life,
TO PUT OFF YOUR OLD SELF,
which is being corrupted by its deceitful desires.

Ephesians 4:22

Wherever the devil has a

FOOTHOLD

in your life something has to go.
Either the foot or the hold; either you
lose part of yourself or you escape.

Dave Davidson

DO NOT GIVE THE DEVIL A FOOTHOLD.

Ephesians 4:27

But among you there MUST NOT BE EVEN A HINT
of sexual immorality, or of any kind of impurity, or of
greed, because THESE ARE IMPROPER for God's holy people.

Ephesians 5:3

*Our culture's rates of divorce,
out-of-wedlock pregnancy,
sexually transmitted
diseases, and devastated relationships
each bear witness to the prevailing
sexual ethic and the consequences of*
abandoning God's call
to sexual purity.

Jerry Kirk

FOR IT IS SHAMEFUL EVEN TO MENTION
WHAT THE DISOBEDIENT DO IN SECRET.

Ephesians 5:12

Wholeness will come when you acknowledge
your part in the failure of your marriage however
unintentional it may have been — and
ALLOW GOD TO TRANSFORM YOU
so you don't end up in the same situation again.

Sharon Marshall

Honor the band on your left hand.

Dan & Dave Davidson

Wives, submit to your husbands as to the Lord. . . . Husbands, love your
wives, just as Christ loved the church and gave himself up for her.

Ephesians 5:22–25

Put on the FULL ARMOR OF GOD so that you
can take your stand against the devil's schemes. . . .
Therefore put on the full armor of God, so that
when the day of evil comes, you may be able to

STAND YOUR GROUND,

and after you have done everything, to stand.

STAND FIRM THEN,

with the belt of truth buckled around your waist,
with the breastplate of righteousness in place,

Ephesians 6:11–14

BETTER TO SHUN THE BAIT THAN STRUGGLE IN THE SNARE.

John Dryden

Pleasure is as difficult to pursue as the end of a rainbow. Look for pleasure and you will *never* find it. Whenever you try to seize it by the tail, it eludes you . . . for *pleasure is a by-product,* a side effect. It takes us by surprise when we are looking for something else. *Seek God* and you find, among other things, piercing pleasure. Seek pleasure and in the long run you find boredom, disillusionment, and enslavement.

John White

Finally, brothers, whatever is true, whatever is noble, whatever is right, whatever is pure, whatever is lovely, whatever is admirable — if anything is excellent or praiseworthy — think about such things.

Philippians 4:8

Put to death, therefore,
whatever belongs to your earthly nature:
sexual immorality, impurity, lust, evil desires
and greed, which is idolatry.

Colossians 3:5

Imagine your dreamiest daydream, your steamiest fantasy, the forbidden thought that has crossed your mind. Picture this whim over and finished and ask yourself

was it worth it?

Would it be worth the consequences, the heartache, and the humiliation?
Would it be worth hurting those you love in the process and the devastation that comes with it? If not, then you'd better stop thinking about it.

Dave Davidson

Set your minds on things above, not on earthly things.

Colossians 3:2

How to Combat Temptation

Recognize the Roar

The devil is described as a roaring lion. God's Word urges us to be alert. Be alert instead of ignorant, devoted rather than deceived, cautious rather than careless. Be watchful and wise as we claim Christ's victory on the cross.

Resist and Remind

The Bible tells us to "resist the devil and he will flee from you." You have to take the step. Say this prayer, *Jesus, in your name I ask you to conquer the devil's strategy right now.* Remind yourself who you are in the Lord. Fix your heart on Jesus and focus your eyes on heaven.

Replace and Rejoice

Rejoice in the Lord. Recite Scripture, sing a hymn, and meditate on God's powerful provision. Replace evil with good. Fill your life with activities and godly thoughts that are praiseworthy and edifying.

Dave Davidson

119

Lust is like a police car
with sirens and flashing lights.
After investigation you're either
free to go or taken in.

Dan Davidson

Bear with each other and forgive whatever grievances you may have
against one another. Forgive as the Lord forgave you.
And over all these virtues put on love, which binds
them all together in perfect unity.

Colossians 3:13–14

I was afraid that in some way the tempter
might have tempted you.

1 Thessalonians 3:5

CLEAN UP YOUR HARD DRIVE!
REBOOT AND RENEW YOUR MIND IN CHRIST.

Dan Davidson

"Oh I want to sin with you, strip away your self-worth and then violate you until you lose your dignity. I want to have my way with you and then leave you with feelings of guilt, bitterness, and resentment."

NOT A GOOD PICKUP LINE!
Sounds stupid, right? Well, it's just as stupid when you do it.

Dave Davidson

For God did not call us to be impure but to
LIVE A HOLY LIFE.
1 Thessalonians 4:7

So then, let us not be like others, who are asleep,
but let us be alert and self-controlled.

1 Thessalonians 5:6

But since we belong to the day,
LET US BE SELF-CONTROLLED,
putting on faith and love as a breastplate,
and the hope of salvation as a helmet.

1 Thessalonians 5:8

Preventing Future Falls

From the corner of my eye, I noticed a cabinet full of glass lamp fixtures start to fall. My four-year-old son, Nathan, had accidentally tipped it forward toward his one-year-old brother, Joshua, who was playing in front of it.

I watched, horrified, as the cabinet seemed to stop in mid-air, hanging diagonally to the floor. Even the light fixtures dodged Joshua as they bounced around him. Was this my imagination or a miracle?

The cabinet was indeed suspended, thanks to a bungee cord that I had attached years earlier from the cabinet to the ceiling. Praise the Lord! The boys were safe. To my relief, God had given me wisdom to take preventative measures to protect my family from potential danger.

Consider your purity in the same way. The more boundaries and safety nets you put in place now, the easier it will be for you to remain pure. In the future, when you've successfully avoided temptation because of decisions you make and commit to today, you and your family will be praising the Lord, too!

Dave Davidson

IT IS GOD'S WILL

**that you should be sanctified:
that you should avoid sexual immorality;
that each of you should learn to control his own body
in a way that is holy and honorable, not in passionate
lust like the heathen, who do not know God.**

1 Thessalonians 4:3–5

GOD,

the God of the Bible,
IS NOT A PRUDE!

He is extremely pro-sex! He's all for

sex — within the parameters of marriage.

Joshua Harris

Today's teens are under a lot of pressure
and are being forced to make a lot of big decisions
early in life — especially when it comes to sexuality.
I am a virgin, and I'm proud of it.
I've made that commitment to God and to my
future husband — whoever that may be.

Rebecca St. James

Avoid circumstances where compromise is likely. . . .
Sexual contact between a boy and a girl is a progressive thing.
The amount of touching, caressing, and kissing that occurs in
the early days tends to increase . . . this progression must be
consciously resisted by Christian young people who want
to serve God and live by His standards.

James Dobson

Flee from flesh, focus on faith.

Dan Davidson

At no time in history has our society been more in need of men willing to STAND UP, BE DIFFERENT, and DEMONSTRATE THE JOY OF LIVING by a fundamentally better standard.

Jerry Kirk

Don't let anyone look down on you
BECAUSE YOU ARE YOUNG,
but set an example for the believers
in speech, in life, in love, in faith and in purity.

1 Timothy 4:12

**Watch your life and doctrine closely.
Persevere in them, because if you do, you
will save both yourself and your hearers.**

1 Timothy 4:16

Hang-ups happen

when we rationalize and deny the habits we contemplate.

For example, God doesn't condone homosexuality or homophobia.

One is of the body, the other of the mind; both are of the heart.

Dave Davidson

**Do not share in the sins of others.
KEEP YOURSELF PURE.**

1 Timothy 5:22

The most significant accomplishments of
transformation in human life involves
TRAINING, NOT SIMPLY TRYING.
It must become a way of life. This simply has
to do with arranging your life around God.

John Ortberg

HYPOCRITE:

Someone who complains that there's too much sex and violence on his VCR.

Anonymous

But you, man of God, flee from all this, and pursue
righteousness, godliness, faith, love, endurance, and gentleness.
FIGHT THE **GOOD FIGHT** OF THE FAITH.

1 Timothy 6:11–12

Suppose You Are a Prostitute

One day you hear that the king has decreed that all prostitutes are forgiven. Since you're a prostitute, that's great news! But would it necessarily change your behavior or your self-perception? Probably not. You may dance in the streets for a while, but chances are you would continue in your same vocation. You would see yourself as nothing more than a forgiven prostitute.

Now suppose the king not only forgave you, but he made you his bride as well. You're a queen. Would that change your behavior? Of course. Why would you want to live as a prostitute if you were a queen?

The Church is the bride of Christ! You are far more likely to promote the Kingdom if you are the queen rather than a forgiven prostitute. We are not redeemed caterpillars; we are butterflies. Why would you want to crawl in some false humility when you are called to mount up with wings as eagles?

Neil Anderson

CAN YOU SAY THIS TO GOD?

I really believe if we're going to be serious about living sold-out for God, we need to say, *I do not want to fill my mind with the junk that's out there.* I don't want to waste my time putting things into my brain that I won't be able to get out.

Rebecca St. James

Do your best to present yourself to God as one approved, a workman who does not need to be ashamed and who correctly handles the word of truth.

2 Timothy 2:15

Past sin, truly repented, is forgiven by God. Don't let Satan bring you down with constant reminders of it. You can be brand new in Christ.

Angie Cundiff

130

FLEE THE EVIL DESIRES OF YOUTH,

and pursue righteousness, faith, love
and peace, along with those who call
on the Lord out of a pure heart.

2 Timothy 2:22

**For the grace of God that brings salvation has
appeared to all men. It teaches us to say "No" to
ungodliness and worldly passions, and to live
self-controlled, upright, and godly lives in this
present age, while we wait for the blessed hope.**

Titus 2:11–13

Jesus, on temptation and sin:
Been There,
Not Done That.

Dave Davidson

**Because he himself suffered when he was tempted,
he is able to help those who are being tempted.**

Hebrews 2:18

**For we do not have a high priest who is unable to
sympathize with our weaknesses, but we have one who has been
tempted in every way, just as we are — yet was without sin.**

Hebrews 4:15

A healthy self-image

is seeing yourself as God sees you
no more and no less.

Josh McDowell

A PURITY COVENANT FOR ENGAGED COUPLES

In obedience to God's command, I promise to protect
your moral purity from this day until our honeymoon.
Because I respect and honor you, I commit to build up the
inner person of your heart rather than violate you. I pledge
to show my love for you in ways that allow both of us to
maintain a clear conscience before God and each other.

Dennis & Barbara Rainey

We have this hope as an
ANCHOR FOR THE SOUL,
firm and secure.

Hebrews 6:19

Faithfulness requires

total love and devotion to God and to your spouse.
Faithfulness is built upon a foundation of sacrificial love
that honors your partner more than yourself.

Dan Davidson

MARRIAGE

should be honored by all,
and the marriage bed kept pure.

Hebrews 13:4

Lonely people often feel that God
does not care for them. You're already special enough
for Jesus to die for you, but you're not special enough for God
to lie about His love for you. If God was a liar the universe
would crumble. The truth is God does love you
and He is close to the brokenhearted

Dave Davidson

CONSIDER IT PURE JOY,

my brothers, whenever you face trials of many kinds,
because you know that the testing of your faith
develops perseverance.

James 1:3

When you are thirsty
do you drink paint?
In the same way, don't react hastily in
self-destructive ways regarding morality.

Dave Davidson

LUST IS NOT A CRAVING, A FANCY, OR A WHIM.
IT'S SIN.

T.D. Jakes

When tempted, no one should say, "God is tempting me."
For God cannot be tempted by evil, nor does he tempt anyone;
but each one is tempted when, by his own evil desire, he is dragged
away and enticed. Then, after desire has conceived, it gives birth
to sin; and sin, when it is full-grown, gives birth to death.

James 1:13–15

The Truth about Sin and What to Do about It

Sin deceives, defiles, and destroys. Sin denies, demeans, depraves, debases, and degrades. Sin desires defeat by disguising its devious demands.

Sin derails and demolishes. Sin demoralizes and deviates while dishonoring and disrupting. Sin dissolves, disconnects, and disposes. Sin deadens the downcast and discourages disciples. Sin distorts, distracts, divides, and dissatisfies.

God forbids sin because it is contrary to His perfect will for us. Our avoidance of sin can reflect our love for God, helping us understand who we are in Christ. Our conviction of sin will always be in proportion to our pursuit of God's presence in our lives.

We gain the victory by giving up sin's pleasure for Christ's power. When we confess, God covers all our sins with the blood of His Son, Jesus. God is ready to forgive and restore with His unconditional love for those who repent.

Dave Davidson

THE OLD T-SHIRT THEOLOGY,

THE DEVIL MADE ME DO IT,

isn't exactly the way things happen.
The devil deceives me into thinking sin will satisfy
my needs. Since I haven't learned to trust God enough,
compared to the luring lies of the devil, I decided to do it.
I foolishly bought the lie that sin is fun,
which brings dishonor to the living God.

Dave Davidson

Do not merely L I S T E N to the word,
and so deceive yourselves.
DO WHAT IT SAYS.

James 1:22

Submit yourselves, then, to God.
RESIST THE DEVIL,
and he will flee from you. Come near
to God and he will come near to you.
Wash your hands, you sinners. Purify
your hearts, you double-minded.

James 4:7–8

After each failure, ask forgiveness,
pick yourself up, and try again.
Very often what God first helps us toward is not the virtue
itself, but just the power of always trying again.

C.S. Lewis

LOOPHOLES

are more of a thief of freedom than a means of freedom.
The more you fall for the lie of a loophole, the more it ties
you up. It entangles you. Our first question should be,
"What is best?" not "What can I get by with?"

— Dave Davidson —

Anyone, then, who knows the good
he ought to do and doesn't do it, SINS.

James 4:17

As obedient children, do not conform to the
evil desires you had when you lived in ignorance.

1 Peter 1:14

CAN YOU SAY THIS TO GOD?

I MAKE IT A RULE OF CHRISTIAN DUTY
NEVER TO GO TO A PLACE WHERE THERE IS NOT
ROOM FOR MY MASTER AS WELL AS MYSELF.

John Newton

Dear friends, I urge you, as aliens and strangers
in the world, to ABSTAIN FROM SINFUL DESIRES,
which war against your soul.

1 Peter 2:11

141

LUST is a trick where you act amused with the show even though you know the MAGIC ISN'T REAL.

PREMARITAL SEX is like unwrapping a Christmas gift on Halloween. It is DISAPPOINTING AND HAUNTING.

PETTING and not intending to go further is like a drag strip racer revving up the engine with a few toes delicately pressed on the clutch.

Dave Davidson

We have made resisting temptation some mystical, unreachable, unattainable talent reserved either for the very old or the very pious. Baloney! Saying "no" is something all of us who belong to Christ can do and must do! There's nothing magical about it. You simply put Jesus Christ at the helm of your life and say "No!"

Charles Swindoll

If Satan can't entice
me into sinning, then he will
INTIMIDATE ME
to being disloyal to God through fear.

Kay Arthur

BE SELF-CONTROLLED AND ALERT.
Your enemy the devil prowls around like
a roaring lion looking
for someone to devour.

1 Peter 5:8

Resist him, standing firm in the faith.

1 Peter 5:9

This
DIVINE POWER HAS GIVEN US EVERYTHING
we need for life and godliness
through our knowledge of him who called us
by his own glory and goodness.
Through these he has given us his very great
and precious promises, so that through them
you may participate in the divine nature and escape the
corruption in the world caused by evil desires.

2 Peter 1:3–4

The places we go, the friendships we embrace, the

language we use, the shows we watch, the books we read,

the thoughts we entertain — all must be aligned with

the purpose to which we are called by God.

Ravi Zacharias

Walking In the Light

God is light; in him there is no darkness at all . . . if we walk in the light,
as he is in the light, we have fellowship with one another,
and the blood of Jesus, his Son, purifies us from all sin.
1 John 1:5–7

Imagine hiking with friends on a beautiful summer day. You leave the trail and walk directly into a prison cell made of solid concrete blocks. Once inside, the door closes itself and you are in total darkness.

For a moment you start to panic and think you're trapped. Why did you walk into this dark damp cell anyway? What will you tell others about your decision to leave and walk away from the light of day?

Finally, you realize that the door has no lock and you walk out just as easily as you entered. Soon, you are back walking in the light.

Our Christian walk of faith is always in the light because God is light. The enemy may try to convince us to walk into dungeons of darkness, but on the cross Christ destroyed the gates to hell, enabling us to escape any temptation we are faced with. Commit today to walk in the light of the Lord!

Dan Davidson

Never minimize sin.
NEVER MAXIMIZE SIN.
Repent the sin for what it is,
MOVE ON WITH GOD.
GET OVER IT!

Dave Davidson

WHEN GOD FORGIVES HE FORGETS.
He buries our sins in the sea and puts a sign on the bank, "No Fishing Allowed."

Corrie Ten Boom

If we confess our sins, he is faithful and just and will forgive
us our sins and purify us from all unrighteousness.

1 John 1:9

Everyone who has this hope in him
purifies himself, just as he is pure.

1 John 3:3

*The Christian mortifies the flesh by submitting
to the authority of Christ . . . including his God-given
but very dangerous sexuality. It's as dangerous as dynamite.
Fire and water, too, are gifts of God, but when they*

GET OUT OF CONTROL,
the result is devastation.

Elizabeth Elliot

Let us not love with words or tongue but with
actions and in truth.

1 John 3:18

BEAUTY
IS THE GIFT OF GOD.

Aristotle

When a trapeze artist is about to jump,
he's making two commitments.

He's committing to release the trapeze and to grab the catcher.

Without both commitments he'll fall. The same is true of us.

We must let go of our sin and turn to God.

Bill Perkins

The world and its desires pass away,
but the man who does the will of God
LIVES FOREVER.

1 John 2:17

Pornography distorts reality, devalues sex, and
CREATES ISOLATION.
It never satisfies and always leaves you wanting more.
It destroys a spouse's self-esteem, kills careers, feeds organized
crime, and facilitates child molestation. Pornography grieves
the heart of God and gives Satan a stronghold in your life.

adapted from Henry Rogers

Dear children, keep yourselves from idols.

1 John 5:21

GOD CAN'T GIVE US HAPPINESS AND PEACE APART FROM HIMSELF,
because it is not there. There is no such thing.

C.S. Lewis

When exploring Temptation Island it's hard to tell
the difference between climbing a mountain or a volcano
BEFORE IT'S TOO LATE.
You can certainly wind up a singed castaway.

Dave Davidson

Those whom I love I rebuke and
discipline. So be earnest, and repent.

Revelation 3:19

F.O.R.G.I.V.E.N.E.S.S. S.T.E.P.

Figure out exactly what is hurting. Psalm 139:23–24

Observe and understand in light of the Cross. Luke 23:34

Resolve to forgive by Christ's power within you. Matthew 9:6

Give God permission to control all emotional change. Matthew 6:12–15

Identify new positive ways to look at the situation. Romans 8:28

Verify in your own heart that God will take care of it. Ezekiel 16:62–63

Erase what is owed to you as you release responsibility. Matthew 18:27

Never return to your old perspective despite feelings. 1 John 2:12

Eliminate grudges and forgive as you pray. Mark 11:25

Stop further sin with restoration. James 5:20

Saturate yourself in the truth of God's mercy. Titus 3:4–5

Start the healing with God's comfort. 2 Corinthians 1:3, 4

Take responsibility for your fault, blame or part. 1 John 1:9

Expect to be patient with yourself and others. Colossians 3:12–14

Praise God for His victory over sin. Romans 4:7–8

Dave Davidson

151

Think WOW Purity Plan

Think WOW: Purity is not only possible, it is God's plan and provision for you. What if you took this to heart and saved sex for marriage? God can make your heart brand new and pure, whether you are married or single. (See 1 John 3:3)

Make A VOW: Maintaining sexual purity requires a strong commitment. Make a purity pledge to yourself, to God, your spouse or to your future spouse. Devote your heart to God and promise to remain faithful. (See 1 John 1:9)

Plan HOW: Create a plan for self-control. Identify your weaknesses and develop a strategy for accountability. Recognize patterns and habits that make you vulnerable to sin. Be alert and stay plugged into Gods Word. (See 1 John 1:7)

Do It NOW: Decide to follow God's Word for purity today. Stand strong regardless of what others do and say. Be faithful with a purity promise before God. Accept God's forgiveness and know you are His child. (See 1 John 3:18)

Push the PLOW: Continue to meet the daily challenge of purity. Pray for perseverance and hope in God. Never give up, even when you stumble. Make your life a testimony. Produce the fruit of self-control in your life. (See 1 John 2:17)

Dan & Dave Davidson

	S P I R I T	
F	↓ SUSTAIN	↓ STARVE
L		
E → FAMISH	I (Devotion)	III (Depletion)
S		
H → FEED	II (Destruction)	IV (Depravity)

Take a moment to review the Spirit-Flesh zones. Which one best describes your life? If you are a believer, you can re-commit your life to Christ today. Make a personal purity pledge to God on the next page. Promise to live according to God's Word with wholehearted devotion. To survive temptation you must be plugged into the power of Christ on the cross. Do you know Jesus as your personal Savior? If not, you can verify your eternal address in heaven today. The following pages outline God's plan of salvation including a prayer asking Jesus to be Lord of your life.

P.U.R.I.T.Y. PLEDGE

PROMISE
I will promise to keep pure by living God's Word.

UNDERSTAND
I will seek to understand God's design for my love life.

REPENT
I will repent from sin and turn away from temptation.

INITIATE
I will initiate prayer, accountability, and study of God's Word.

TRUST
I will place my trust in God and His plan for my life.

YIELD
I will yield to Christ, surrendering my heart, mind, and soul.

Dan & Dave Davidson

155

HereToHeaven.com

CHASE *We all chase the wind with a heart of sin.*
Ecclesiastes 1:14; Proverbs 14:12; Romans 3:11

SPACE *Sin has put a space between us and God's face.*
Romans 3:23, 6:23; Proverbs 14:12; Isaiah 1:18, 59:2; John 14:6

ERASE *God gave up His only Son to erase sin's debt for everyone.*
John 3:16; 1 Peter 2:24; Isaiah 53:6; Acts 3:19; John 1:12; Galatians 2:20

EMBRACE *Admit your sins and believe; embrace Jesus and receive.*
Romans 5:1-2, 6:8, 10:9-11; Acts 4:12, 10:43; Hebrews 11:1

GRACE *God's grace shown to man is His eternal life plan.*
Ephesians 2:8-9; 1 John 1:9; John 5:24; Titus 3:4-5; Colossians 1:13

REPLACE *Let God replace your debt of sin, then your new life can begin.*
2 Corinthians 5:17; Ephesians 4:24; 1 John 1:7; John 3:36

PLACE *God has a place for us in heaven when we trust.*
John 14:2; 1 Peter 1:3-4; Hebrews 11:10; Revelation 21:1-7

Dan & Dave Davidson

A PRAYER FOR A PURE HEART

Dear God,

I admit that I have sinned against You. I need Your forgiveness. I want to turn away from the sin that separates us and repent. I'm convinced that when Jesus died He took the punishment I deserved for my sins. I know that only Jesus can clean me, erase my sin debt, and replace my old heart with a new pure heart.

I thankfully accept Your wonderful provision of eternal life. I gladly receive Your gift of grace and by faith I believe in Jesus. You are my Lord and my Shepherd. I want to be Your child and live in heaven forever. Thanks for revealing Your great love for me.

I commit my life to serving You. I want to glorify You and live my life as a "thank you" for Your gift of salvation. Help me to understand the depth and richness of Your love. Help me to know You, fear You, follow You, and live in awe of You. Thank You for preparing a place for me in heaven, my faithful God, my Father.

Brothers **DAN AND DAVE DAVIDSON**
share the same mission statement in the acronym
T.I.M.E. — to Teach, Inspire, Motivate, and
Encourage. They have written 20 books
together including *8 P. R.O.M.I.S.E.S.* and
A Cup of Devotion with God.

Dan is a chiropractor in Virginia and Dave
is a photographer in Iowa.
They are both inspirational speakers and record Scripture songs for
PoetTree.com. Dan and his wife, Kimberly, have three children.
Dave and his wife, Joan, have two children.

Join their FREE daily e-mail newsletters at DailyPurity.com,
DailyDevotion.com, DailyMissions.com, DailyRomance.com
and VerseRehearse.com. For a current list of their books and
free online resources visit their websites:
DanDavidson.com and DaveDavidson.com

158

GEORGE VERWER is passionate about encouraging people to live their life for Jesus. He is the founder and international coordinator of Operation Mobilization, a ministry of evangelism, discipleship training, and church planting. He's committed to recruiting missionaries and encouraging churches to follow the example in Acts 13.

He and his wife, Drena, have three adult children and live in England. George is the author of several books including *Out of the Comfort Zone*, and *God's Great Ambition,* co-authored with Dan and Dave Davidson. For more information please visit **GeorgeVerwer.com**.

SurvivingTemptation.com

STAY ACCOUNTABLE
and let this message continue to encourage you!
Sign up for our FREE e-mail newsletter about purity and other resources.

You've read the book, now hear the soundtrack,
"Surviving Temptation Island."
Free song downloads available at PoetTree.com

Many of the Bible verses in this book are the lyrics to the songs.